# Estate Planning

# Overview

## Robert W. Ramsdell

THOMPSON RAMSDELL & QUALSETH, P.A.
333 West 9th Street, Lawrence, Kansas 66044
(785) 841-4554 // Robert.Ramsdell@trqlaw.com
Website: http://trqlaw.com

# DEDICATION
# &
# ACKNOWLEDGEMENT

Dedicated to my wife, Leslie.

I would like to acknowledge the assistance of Michael Carlisle, Joe Karnes, Matt Neis, and David Samms in either reviewing and commenting upon draft versions of this book or discussing its central concepts. Any lack of clarity that remains is my responsibility.

# CONTENTS

# FOREWORD

This book is an outgrowth of the "Fundamentals of Estate Planning" presentation I give at the Douglas County Senior Center, community libraries, and to various groups. It discusses the major factors to consider in making estate planning decisions and the documents that can implement your choices.

I practice as an estate planning attorney in Kansas. Therefore, the specific requirements stated in the text are based on Kansas law. However, the general concepts – such as the types of testamentary trusts, factors to consider in selecting trustees, agents, guardians, etc. – will be of use to anyone.

I have attempted to balance thoroughness with brevity. The result is an emphasis on broad principles applicable to most people while omitting nuances and variations. But there can be more than just the devil in the details – sometimes there is just what you need for your unique situation. The broad principles will provide a starting point if there is a particular issue on which you want more information.

My use of the word brevity should probably be in quote marks. This book increased in length as I revised and edited it, adding material for context and completeness. If a section seems inapplicable to you – such as the discussion about selecting a guardian if you do not have minor children – then scan or skip over it. If something is confusing, write a question in the margin or the notes section at the back and discuss it with someone knowledgeable.

Do not allow choices to paralyze you: "Who should we name as our children's guardian?" "Should we do separate trusts for them or a common trust?" "Who should I name as my healthcare agent?" Neither a drunk crossing the highway centerline nor a heart attack will pause to ask if your estate planning is complete. At the moment it matters, it either will be or not.

So take action. My last assignment in the Army was teaching tactics at the Command & General Staff College where we had a saying: "Failing to plan is planning to fail." Do not let this be you.

Although the information in this book is current as of February 2013, the law may change. This information is provided with the understanding that it is intended to provide general public information, not legal advice. Anyone referring to this information is responsible for determining the current status of the relevant law and its application to their situation, particularly as the emphasis of this book is on general rules to which there may be exceptions.

# DO YOU NEED A PLAN?

Yes.

If you die without a Will, Revocable Living Trust, or some other provision for the distribution of your property, who gets it and the share they receive is determined by the Kansas laws on intestate succession. This may or may not be what you want.

For example, if you die leaving a surviving spouse and children or issue, one-half goes to your surviving spouse and the other half goes to your surviving children or issue, per stirpes. Would you really want your 2-year-old child to receive half of your probate estate (with the possible need for a conservatorship) if your spouse survives you and is capable of continuing to raise your child?

That said, some people may get by without a Will or Trust. A person without minor children has no need to nominate a guardian. A person without significant assets – particularly no real estate or other property for which a clear record of title is needed – may expect his or her heirs to simply agree on how to divide things up (and not care if they can't). And some assets can be distributed through the use of non-testamentary transfers.

But most people would benefit themselves and those they leave behind by having a Will or Trust. These include:

- Anyone who is the parent of a minor child and wants to nominate the person(s) to serve as guardian and raise the child.

- Anyone who wants to create a testamentary trust for their minor child in order to specify the purposes for distributions (education, not three motorcycles at 18), provide for multiple distributions of principal (so the child can do better with the second if he or she blows the first), and include spendthrift provisions to protect the assets from the child's creditors or spouse.

- Anyone who wants to create a Special Needs Trust for an incapacitated child of any age that preserves the child's access to Medicaid and other public benefit programs.

- Anyone who wants to give differing shares to their children based upon their circumstances.

- Anyone in a blended family who has assets they want to ensure ultimately pass to certain persons; for example, by making their current spouse the lifetime income beneficiary of a trust with the assets passing to their children upon the spouse's death.

- Anyone who wants to make charitable bequests, or bequests to friends and family members who fall outside the provisions of intestate succession.

- Anyone in a non-traditional relationship wanting to leave property to a significant other not recognized as their spouse under Kansas law, and who therefore would not receive anything under the laws of intestate succession.

- Anyone who is a business owner and wants to include provisions that mesh with an existing business succession plan or create incentives for a child to continue the business.

The reasons for having a Will or Trust can be as varied and unique as the person for whom it is created. The value of a well-drafted Will or Trust is its flexibility to accomplish many of the things that might be important to you after your death.

Another concern is the possibility of incapacity prior to death. This could occur over time as you age, or quite suddenly if a severe accident leaves you impaired. If you are incapacitated, who do you want to have authority to handle your financial affairs and make medical treatment decisions for you? And if your medical condition becomes terminal, what are your preferences for end-of-life care?

A Durable General Power of Attorney or provision for a successor trustee in a Trust can provide continuity for your financial affairs. A Durable Healthcare Power of Attorney and Living Will & Healthcare Directive can do the same for your medical issues.

The key is to think about what you want to accomplish – both after your death and in the event of your incapacity – and be sure you have a plan in place to make it happen.

# ESTATE & GIFT TAXES

The federal estate tax affects very few people. Even without any tax planning or the use of special deductions, an individual dying in 2013 can transfer up to $5,250,000 of property tax free. A married couple could die and transfer up to $10,500,000 tax free. For most people, the tax implications and other effects of gifts given while living are of more importance. The following discussion is a very brief overview of potentially complicated tax issues and omits a variety of topics, such as the Generation Skipping Transfer Tax, valuation discounts on gifts of minority business interests, etc.

The tax law enacted in early January 2013 kept the $5 million federal estate tax exclusion adopted in 2011 with annual adjustments for inflation. Thus, the exclusion in effect for deaths occurring in 2013 is $5,250,000. Taxable estates in excess of this exclusion amount are taxed at a progressive rate starting at 18% and reaching 40% for all of the excess amount over $1,000,000. (In other words, absent any tax planning or the use of special deductions, the estate tax starts when your estate exceeds $5,250,000 and reaches the maximum 40% rate once your estate exceeds $6,250,000.)

For tax purposes, the assets of a decedent are valued either as of the date of death or, at the executor's option, at their value six months after the date of death if that will result in a lower gross estate and a lower aggregate tax. If certain requirements are met, farm and business property may be valued at its use value if that is less than its fair market value.

For the person receiving property from a decedent, his or her basis is generally its fair market value on the date of death or on the alternate or special use valuation date. For example, assume your father bought 1,000 shares of XYZ Corporation at $10 each many years ago when it was a small technology start-up. The XYZ shares were trading at $1,000 per share on the date of his death and this is the valuation date used.

- Had your father not died but sold all of his shares that day, his $1,000,000 gross proceeds would have included $990,000 in taxable long-term capital gains after subtracting his $10,000 basis.

- Since he died, the $1,000,000 for the shares is included in the value of his estate, which may be subject to estate tax depending upon its total value.

- But your basis becomes the $1,000 per share used to value the stock for the estate. Assume you sell all the shares more than a year after your father's death at $1,025 per share. You would only have $25,000 in taxable long-term capital gains after subtracting your $1,000,000 basis from the $1,025,000 in gross proceeds.

There is an unlimited marital deduction for property left to a spouse who is a U.S. citizen (or becomes one by the time the federal estate tax return is filed). Thus, Bill Gates could leave everything to Melissa – say $50 billion or so – and there would not be a penny of estate tax due on that transfer. (Absent other planning, there would be a huge tax bill if Melissa later died with $50 billion in property. But see the unlimited charitable deduction discussed below.) There is no marital deduction allowed for a non-U.S. citizen spouse unless the property is placed in a Qualified Domestic Trust or is otherwise governed by an applicable tax treaty with the nation of the spouse's citizenship.

There is also an unlimited deduction for property transferred to public, religious, charitable, scientific, literary, and educational organizations that meet certain criteria under the tax code. As a result, Bill and Melissa Gates, Warren Buffett, and a number of other wealthy individuals have announced their intent to leave the bulk of their property to qualified charities as a means of avoiding the estate tax.

The estate tax exclusion is unified with the gift tax such that this amount may be used while living or at death, with any lifetime use subtracted to determine the amount remaining for use at death. For example, if you had previously given $1,000,000 to each of your three children and died in 2013, you would have an unused exclusion of $2,250,000 ($5,250,000 minus the $3,000,000 used for gifts) available for use at your death.

Speaking of gifts, you can give unlimited gifts to a spouse who is a U.S. citizen or up to $143,000 per year (the 2013 limit, with the amount of the annual exclusion in future years to be adjusted for inflation) to a non-U.S. citizen spouse. The annual exclusion amount in 2013 for gifts to anyone other than a spouse is $14,000 (with future limits adjusted for inflation). If you give a gift to a person in excess of that amount, you need to file a gift tax return. Presuming the excess does not exceed your remaining lifetime unified exclusion, no tax will be due – but that amount will not be available for the exclusion at your death, as noted above. Married couples may use "gift splitting" to give up to $28,000 to a person before needing to file a gift tax return.

You can give annual gifts to as many people as you want. If you have three children, six grandchildren, and really appreciate the prompt service of the pizza delivery driver, you can give $14,000 each to all ten of them – moving $140,000 out of your estate – without owing any gift tax or using any of your unified estate / gift tax exclusion.

If you receive a gift from a living donor, your basis is generally the same as the property would be in the hands of the donor. Going back the 1,000 shares of XYZ Corporation, if your father had given these to you while he was living on a day when they were trading at $1,000 per share, that would have been a $1,000,000 gift on which your father would either have owed gift tax or used a portion of his unified estate / gift tax exclusion. But your basis would be the $10 per share basis the stock had while in your father's hands. If you sell all of it at $1,000 per share, you will have a taxable gain of $990,000 out of the $1,000,000 in gross proceeds just as your father would have had.

Section 529 of the tax code not only authorizes tax-advantaged state sponsored qualified savings plans for higher education (imaginatively called "529 Plans"), but also allows a donor to prorate contributions in excess of the annual exclusion amount over a period of five years. So you could make a lump sum contribution of up to $70,000 ($140,000 if gift-split with your spouse) to a grandchild's 529 Plan account in 2013 and owe no gift tax by pro-rating it over the five years from 2013 to 2017. However, if you give the maximum $70,000 in 2013, then any additional gifts to that grandchild over that 5-year period would be taxable (or require the use of a portion of your unified estate / gift tax exclusion) unless the annual exclusion amount increases.

The law provides an unlimited gift tax exclusion for amounts paid for tuition directly to an educational organization for the benefit of another. (Payments for books, room and board, etc. are not eligible for the special tuition exclusion, but would be counted against the annual gift exclusion applicable to that beneficiary.) Similarly, amounts paid directly to healthcare providers for medical services provided to another qualify for an unlimited gift tax exclusion.

A plan of lifetime gifting at or below the annual exclusion amount can be an effective way to transfer assets without paying gift tax or using any of your unified estate / gift tax exclusion. However, if you have a significant reversal of fortune or are simply a person of more modest means to begin with, past gifts can have an adverse impact if you ever need to qualify for Medicaid to pay for long-term nursing care. See the discussion at the end of the chapter on Revocable Living Trusts.

The federal estate tax retains the portability provision that began in 2011. This allows the unused exclusion amount of the first-to-die spouse (called the deceased spousal unused exclusion amount or DSUEA) to be used by the surviving spouse (in addition to his or her own exclusion) at their death. A key requirement is that a federal estate tax return must be filed in a timely manner to compute and elect taking the DSUEA even if a tax return is otherwise not needed.

For example, Frank and Kathy are married. Kathy dies in 2013, having previously given $1,000,000 to each of their three children. At her death, Kathy's estate had a value of $4,000,000, exceeding her unused exclusion of $2,250,000 ($5,250,000 minus the $3,000,000 used for gifts), but she left all of her remaining property to Frank (a U.S. citizen) such that it is covered by the unlimited marital deduction and no estate tax is due. If the executor files a timely federal estate tax return that computes and elects taking Kathy's DSUEA, then when Frank dies his estate can use the combined amount of Kathy's $2,250,000 DSUEA plus his own unused unified estate / gift tax exclusion based upon the inflation-adjusted amount in effect during the year of his death.

Black widows / widowers need not apply. The law limits the surviving spouse's estate to using the DSUEA of the "last such deceased spouse." So a person cannot collect and add together unused exclusion amounts from multiple deceased spouses.

The availability of portability may lessen the need for a Bypass Trust (also called a Credit Shelter Trust) for some couples. However, unlike leaving assets outright to a surviving spouse, a Bypass Trust provides asset protection should the surviving spouse remarry, then divorce, and may allow the first-to-die spouse to control the ultimate distribution of the trust's assets upon the death of the surviving spouse.

Although typically used to provide for a surviving spouse, anyone could be the beneficiary of a Bypass Trust. The value of the assets used to fund the Bypass Trust is counted against the decedent's exclusion amount. The beneficiary may then be given extensive rights without the assets of the Trust being included in the beneficiary's taxable estate. These rights may include:

- The right to income from the Trust for life.

- The right to have an independent trustee invade the principal of the Trust for the beneficiary's benefit.

- The right of the beneficiary to withdraw the greater of $5,000 or 5% of the Trust's principal per year.

- The right of the beneficiary to principal from the Trust in accordance with an ascertainable standard relating to health, education, maintenance or support.

- A limited power of appointment, exercisable during life or on death, to appoint the Trust's remaining principal to any person or entity other than the beneficiary, his or her estate, his or her creditors, or the creditors of his or her estate. For example, the first-to-die spouse could create a Bypass Trust for the benefit of the surviving spouse that initially provides for the remainder to pass in equal shares to their children.

The surviving spouse might be given a limited power of appointment to alter the shares of the children in response to changed circumstances (such as the unforeseen medical expenses of a child severely injured after the death of the first-to-die spouse).

Looking back at Frank and Kathy, once Kathy left her $4,000,000 of property outright to Frank, it was his. He can leave it to his and Kathy's three children, or not. If he remarries and dies before his new spouse, Rachel, he can leave it all to her. Or, if he and Rachel divorce, then absent a premarital agreement that property is on the table for the divorce settlement. However, if Kathy had left $1,500,000 outright to Frank while placing the other $2,500,000 in a Bypass Trust of which he was the lifetime beneficiary with her three children the remainder beneficiaries, then at least the remaining balance of the Bypass Trust would go to Kathy's children regardless of what Frank does following her death.

A word of warning: If you have a Will or Living Trust drafted a number of years ago that includes a Bypass Trust, you should have its terms reviewed carefully as many Bypass Trusts are funded – prior to anything going outright to the surviving spouse or anyone else – by a formula such as "in an amount equal to the amount of the applicable exclusion amount available by reason of my unused Unified Tax Credit under the Internal Revenue Code." Since future amounts of the exclusion are unknown when a Will or Living Trust is drafted, the purpose of such a formula is to maximize the estate tax savings by funding the Bypass Trust with the decedent's assets up to the full exclusion amount in effect during the year of their death.

However, this can leave little to your surviving spouse or others if your assets have not grown as fast as the exclusion. For example, say you had a gross estate of $2,000,000 and died in 2001 when the exclusion amount was $1,000,000. The above formula would have placed $1,000,000 in your Bypass Trust with the other $1,000,000 passing to whoever you designated, most likely your surviving spouse. Now it's 2013. You've done well in the past decade or so, with your $2,000,000 more than doubling to $5,000,000. But if you die this year, the formula will fund the Bypass Trust with the entire $5,000,000, leaving nothing to pass outright to your spouse or whoever else you designated.

On a final note, the Kansas estate tax was repealed effective January 1, 2010. However, if the decedent owned property in other states, then whoever handles their estate must check the estate or inheritance tax laws of the states where the property is located to see if any of those states impose a tax on the property located within them.

# INTESTATE SUCCESSION

If you die without a Will, Revocable Living Trust, or some other provision for the distribution of your property (such as one or more of the non-testamentary transfers discussed later), who gets your property and the share they receive is determined by the Kansas laws on intestate succession.

The statutes of intestate succession specify the priority and shares of your property that go to persons related to you within six degrees of separation. If no one related to you can be located and you had a spouse to whom you were married at the time of such spouse's earlier death, then the law specifies the priority and shares of your property that go to persons related to your predeceased spouse within six degrees of separation. If no one related to you or your predeceased spouse can be located, then your property goes to the State of Kansas.

The distribution under intestate succession may or may not be what you want. For example, if you die leaving a surviving spouse and children or issue, one-half goes to your surviving spouse and the other half goes to your surviving children or issue, per stirpes.

- If young, do you want your 2-year-old child to receive half of your probate estate (with the possible need for a conservatorship) if your spouse survives you and is capable of continuing to raise your child?
  - And then have the remaining assets paid out in a lump sum to the child upon turning 18?

- If older / retired, do you want half of your probate estate to go to your adult children and not your spouse?

The statutes on intestate succession also lack flexibility. For example, presume your spouse died before you and you are survived by two children. Mary is in excellent health and is in the midst of a successful career that has made her wealthy. John was severely injured in an accident as a young adult, cannot work, and needs ongoing, expensive medical care. Under intestate succession, Mary and John will receive equal shares despite their differing circumstances.

While not a common circumstance, some people have surrendered their parental rights. For example, a high school student who gave up her baby for adoption at birth. Or a young man who, after a divorce, allowed their still young children to be adopted by the new husband of his former wife. While you cannot inherit from a child with whom your parental rights are severed, such a child remains your heir under intestate succession. Depending upon the circumstances, you may or may not want such a child to be treated the same as children you subsequently had and raised.

Finally, if you are in a non-traditional relationship where your significant other is not recognized as your spouse under Kansas law, then he or she will not receive any of your property under the laws of intestate succession.

# WILLS

Any person of sound mind, possessing rights of majority, may dispose of any or all of his or her property by Will. The mental capacity ("sound mind") necessary to execute a Will requires that – at the time the Will is executed – you know and understand the nature and extent of your property, have an intelligent understanding of the disposition you desire, realize who are your relatives and the natural objects of your bounty, and comprehend the nature of the claims of those included or excluded in the distribution of your property.

In short, a person may lack the capacity to fully understand a complex contract – such as the lease of an automobile – yet possess the capacity needed to execute a Will.

While Kansas law allows for an oral Will made in a person's last sickness (which is valid only in respect to personal property), every other Will must be in writing and signed at the end by the testator making the Will, or by some other person in the presence of and by the express direction of the testator. The Will must also be attested and subscribed in the presence of the testator by two or more competent witnesses, each of whom saw the testator sign the Will or heard the testator acknowledge the Will. Best practice is to include sworn acknowledgements and affidavits of the testator and attesting witnesses such that the Will is self-proved.

A well-drafted Will can be tailored to your specific desires while having the flexibility to address a variety of contingencies. Highlights of items you can include or address in a Will (or in a Revocable Living Trust, discussed in the next chapter) include the following:

## Specific Devises & Bequests

You can leave specific devises (the term used for real property) or bequests (of other property) of any nature to whatever people or organizations you choose – "My 1972 Gran Torino to my neighbor, Thao" or "$5,000.00 to The Salvation Army."

If you are leaving a large monetary bequest, consider specifying it as "up to $X, not to exceed Y% of my gross estate." This will avoid a bequest from taking an unexpectedly large portion of your estate should your assets at death be less than you expected, whether as a result of years of living expenses or a sudden decline in value such as many assets experienced in 2008.

If you use specific devises and bequests to distribute significant portions of your estate, then update your Will if you sell or dispose of any of the assets constituting them. For example, assume your spouse is deceased and you have two children. Susan, who lives nearby, would love to inherit the family home. Roger, living in New York City, has no interest in the house. Since your other assets are roughly equal in value to the house, you make a specific devise of the house to Susan and leave everything else to Roger. Time passes. You sell the house and move into a retirement community. Unless you update your Will, you have effectively disinherited Susan as there is no longer a house for her to receive as a specific devise.

Also consider what you want to happen to the specific devise or bequest if the named person does not survive you. Kansas law provides that if you make a devise or bequest to a spouse or any relative within the sixth degree and that person dies before you, leaving issue that do survive you, then the surviving issue will take the property unless your Will provides otherwise. For example, assume you did not sell the house, but Susan died before you. If Susan was survived by any descendants, by blood or adoption, then the house will pass to them unless your Will provides otherwise. If Susan had no issue, then the devise will lapse and the house distributed as part of your residuary estate, discussed below.

On the other hand, Thao is neither the spouse nor a relative of Walt Kowalski. If Clint Eastwood rewrites the script such that Walt does not confront the Hmong gang and the gang kills Thao before Walt dies, then the bequest of the Gran Torino to Thao lapses – even if Thao had issue – and the car is distributed as part of the residuary estate unless Walt's Will provided otherwise.

Tangible Personal Property

Your Will may refer to a Written Statement for the Disposition of Tangible Personal Property. This is a list – separate from your Will – of items of tangible personal property (such as a pocket watch, a piece of jewelry or the Ethan Allen dining room set) and the person to whom each item is given. The list must either be in your handwriting or signed by you, and describe each of the items with reasonable certainty. The Will typically directs your executor to search for such a list and honor its instructions; but if no list is found within the time specified by your Will, then the executor is instructed to presume you did not create one.

The great advantage of incorporating a reference to a Written Statement for the Disposition of Tangible Personal Property in your Will is that you do not need to amend your Will each time you wish to modify the disposition of specific items of such property; you simply redo the list. However, the list cannot be used for real estate, properties used in trade or business, documents of title or intangible personal property (such as money, evidences of debt, and securities).

If the balance of your tangible personal property (after any specific bequests and those items disposed of via a written list) is to be divided among a number of people, consider giving guidance on how to handle disputes regarding items that two or more beneficiaries want. For example, you could advise your executor to use an equitable system – such as drawing straws to determine the sequence of picking or the use of a non-monetary, points-based family "auction" – to ensure each person has an equal and fair opportunity to select those items he or she wants.

You should also provide authority for your executor to sell any personal property not wanted by the beneficiaries along with instructions on how the sale proceeds are to be distributed.

## Residuary Estate & Contingent Beneficiaries

While there is no legal limit to the number of specific devises and bequests you make, as a practical matter a Will should have fewer pages than *War and Peace*.

For most people, the preponderance of their property passes as what is called the residuary estate. A typical clause might read: "I devise and bequeath all of the rest, residue, and remainder of my property, real and personal ("my residuary estate"), wherever situated, to ... ...." It is often in the provisions for the residuary estate that testamentary trusts appear. Whether your Will provides for a trust or not, it is very important that you identify contingent beneficiaries if the primary beneficiary(ies) of your residuary estate do not survive you.

Most commonly, people think of family – spouse, children, grandchildren, and others – in distributing their property. But also consider who should receive the assets of your estate if your spouse and children / family are all deceased, or if they fail to live through the term of any trusts that are established for them (the "meteorite hits family reunion" scenario). Such contingent beneficiaries might include anyone or anything significant to you – a charity you supported while living, the school you attended, an organization researching the cure for a disease, a religious institution, a hospital or close friends.

## Per capita vs. Per stirpes

Per capita ("by the heads") gives equal shares to the living members of a class all of whom stand in equal degree to the decedent. A definition of per stirpes ("by representation") might be:

> Any distribution to be made per stirpes under this Will shall be divided into shares in accordance with the number of persons in the generation nearest to me that has one or more then living representatives. Such shares shall be equally divided among those persons in that generation who are then living and those persons in that generation who are then deceased leaving descendants then living. Each then living representative in such generation shall receive one share and each re-maining share shall be allocated in the same manner among the then living descendants of each representative in such generation who is then deceased.

An example will illustrate the differences.

Ann was married to Bob, who has predeceased her. At the time she is preparing her Will, Ann's three children – Charles, David, and Emily – are all living. Charles had a child, Fred, who died in an accident several years ago; David has never had any children; and Emily has two living children, Gerri and Harry. This situation is depicted in the diagram at the top of the next page.

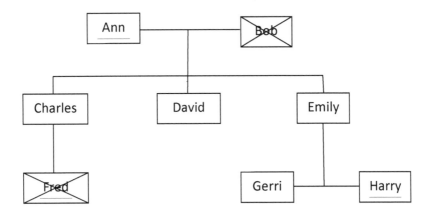

Ann is considering whether to leave certain property "to my children, per capita" or "to my children and their descendents, per stirpes."

Consider the following scenarios regarding situations that might exist at the time of Ann's death:

- Ann is survived by all three children and the two grandchildren – The property goes in one-third shares to Charles, David, and Emily under both per capita and per stirpes.

- Emily predeceases Ann, but Ann is survived by Charles, David, Gerri, and Harry – Under per capita, the property goes in one-half shares to Charles and David. Under per stirpes, the property is split into one-third shares based on the two living members and the one deceased member with living descendents of the generation closest to Ann. Charles and David each get a one-third share. The one-third share that would have gone to Emily flows downstream to her children, with Gerri and Harry each getting a one-sixth share.

- Charles predeceases Ann, but Ann is survived by David, Emily, Gerri and Harry – Under per capita, the property goes in one-half shares to David and Emily. Under per stirpes, the property also goes in one-half shares to David and Emily. (Since Charles left no living descendents, per stirpes only sees the two living members of the generation closest to Ann.)

## Testamentary Trusts

The ability to provide for the creation of testamentary trusts is one of the most powerful attributes of a Will.

Parents of minor children can provide for a trust to be established for their children in the event of the death of the surviving parent or the deaths of both parents. One benefit of a trust is that otherwise any child would be entitled to receive property outright when the child is 18 years of age. In most cases, that would result in a sizable sum of money suddenly being in the control of an 18-year-old who may be more interested in such things as cars and stereos than in obtaining an education or saving for the future. Using a trust allows for some control over the rate and purpose for which the money is spent. A trust may also include a spendthrift provision to keep its assets outside the reach of creditors and a beneficiary's spouse.

The parents can specify a single age at which the trust's principal is to be distributed to the child, or a frequently used safeguard is to provide for at least two distribution dates. For example, the child might receive one-half at age 25 and the remaining balance at age 30 so if the child wastes the first distribution, he or she has a chance to learn from that mistake. Some parents decide to have three distributions (e.g., one-third at age 21, one-half of the remaining balance at age 25, and the remaining balance at age 30). If you opt for a testamentary trust, then it is your decision whether to adopt multiple distributions and, if so, the ages for distributing the trust funds.

Even if you no longer have minor children, depending upon the circumstances you might still consider that your Will provide for a trust to be established for your descendants in the event a child predeceases you and assets pass to one or more minor grandchildren. A trust can also be created for a beneficiary other than a descendant.

You can also give guidance to the trustee as to the purposes for which distributions are to be made. The beneficiary's "health, education, maintenance, and support" is often used as overall guidance, but you could also direct the trustee to consider discretionary distributions to assist with the purchase of a residence, investment in a business or professional activity, or something else you consider worthy of support. In the case of minor children, provision is usually made for additional common family expenses of their guardian.

Also consider whether you want to create a separate trust for each beneficiary or a common trust for multiple beneficiaries. For example, assume you have three children to whom you want to leave assets in trust until they reach a certain age:

- If your Will provides for separate trusts, then three separate trusts will be created and funded at your death (most often in equal shares, although you could specify differing shares) with the assets of each trust subsequently used strictly for the benefit of the child who is its beneficiary. (Think of the assets being divided into three buckets and each child being given a bucket.)

  Separate trusts can simplify the distributions for each beneficiary, particularly distributions of principal at specified ages. However, although the same person or entity might be serving as trustee of all three trusts and your Will may have authorized the commingling for investment purposes of the property of the trusts, the assets of each trust must be used strictly for the child who is the beneficiary of that trust. Should the children's circumstances change – such as one child being severely injured and incurring extensive medical expenses – the trustee cannot alter the trusts' funding or distributions to use the other children's trusts for the benefit of the injured child.

- If your Will provides for a common trust, then a single trust will be created at your death and funded with all the assets. The provisions of the trust then instruct the trustee how to make distributions for the benefit of all three children, typically with discretion to make differing distributions among them as the trustee deems appropriate. (Think of the assets going into one big bucket connected to a hose that the trustee can use to spray benefits on the three children.)

  While creating flexibility for varying distributions as circumstances warrant, a common trust can complicate distributions of principal. For example, if the remaining principal is to be distributed among the children when the youngest child reaches a specified age, then the two older children must wait until they are past that age to receive their shares. This issue is exacerbated as the differences in ages increase.

If you have an incapacitated child of any age whose need for care and financial condition have resulted in their eligibility for Medicaid or other means-tested public benefit programs, then you should consider the creation of a testamentary Special Needs Trust. If such a child simply inherits substantial assets outright, then they are likely to lose their public benefits until the inherited assets are exhausted and they are one again poor enough to qualify.

The provisions of a Special Needs Trust must comply with statutory and regulatory requirements so as not to be considered an asset available to the incapacitated person.

In particular, any distributions must be at the absolute discretion of the trustee; there can be nothing that requires the trustee to make distributions. However, properly crafted, a Special Needs Trust can allow the trustee discretion to supplement the welfare of an incapacitated person – for example, the purchase of a vehicle modified to transport a wheelchair – while preserving that person's eligibility for Medicaid or other means-tested public benefit programs.

Testamentary trusts can also assist planning for blended families. For example, presume you have children from a marriage that ended due to death or divorce, and subsequently remarried. If you leave assets outright to your new spouse, then that spouse can distribute them however they wish at their death – which may or may not include your children. An alternative would be a testamentary trust that names your spouse the lifetime income beneficiary of certain assets – which might include the right to occupy certain property as a residence – with the remaining principal passing to your children at the death of the spouse. (This could be structured as a Bypass Trust, discussed in the chapter on Estate & Gift Taxes, if taxes are a concern but need not be.)

As a variant on the above example, I once had a client without children or descendents who wanted to provide for an adult relative. We crafted a lifetime trust for the benefit of this person with the remaining assets of the trust passing to a charitable entity at their death.

Some assets require special trust provisions. For example, shares in a Subchapter S corporation can only be held by certain forms of trusts or else the S election is nullified and the corporation is taxed as a regular C corporation. Similarly, a trust intended to receive IRA distributions must meet specific requirements to qualify as a "designated beneficiary" under the tax code or else the ability to extend tax-deferred distributions will be lost.

These are simply a few examples of how a testamentary trust might be used. Testamentary trusts can be as varied as the needs and wishes of the person creating them.

One factor to consider, however, are the administrative, investment, and other expenses required for the control and management of a trust. These may be high in relation to the value of assets in a small trust, such as a fractional share passing to a grandchild or further descendent per stirpes. One option is to authorize your executor to distribute such descendant's share under the applicable Uniform Transfers to Minors Act to a custodian designated by the executor if, in the executor's judgment, the amount of assets passing to such descendant do not justify the cost of a trust.

## Selecting a Trustee

The trustee is the person or financial institution that can be anticipated to be available for the entire term of the testamentary trust to make investment decisions, decide upon distributions, pay taxes, and otherwise meet the trust's objectives and requirements.

The Kansas Uniform Trust Code provides that, unless the terms of the trust specify the trustee's compensation, "a trustee is entitled to compensation that is reasonable under the circumstances." Financial institutions typically charge a fee as a percentage of the trust's assets for this service. Some individuals also use a financially savvy relative or friend that they trust, although you need to discuss serving as a trustee with such a person in advance and ensure they are willing to do so.

There is no bright line rule on whether to name an individual or a financial institution as trustee. Factors to consider include:

- The amount and nature of the assets that will be placed in the trust, and the trustee's ability to manage them.

- The ability of the trustee to say "No" (when appropriate) to the beneficiary's request for a discretionary distribution.

- The anticipated duration of the trust, and the trustee's ability to serve for that duration. Contrast a trust for a minor child that will end no later than the child's attainment of a specified age with a special needs trust that may exist for the unknown length of the beneficiary's life.

- The complexity of the trust's distribution provisions, and the trustee's ability to balance competing interests in accordance with the trust's terms. Contrast separate trusts for minor children, each of which has a single beneficiary, with a spray trust for multiple children where the trustee has authority to make differing distributions. Or contrast a separate trust with a single beneficiary whose assets are distributed to the beneficiary's estate if the beneficiary dies before the trust ends to a lifetime trust for the benefit of one beneficiary with one or more other beneficiaries designated to receive the remainder upon the death of the initial beneficiary.

If you name one or more individuals as the initial and successor trustees, then you should name a financial institution as the final back-up trustee just in case the individuals cannot or will not serve for the full duration of the trust.

There are many financial institutions that might serve as a corporate trustee, both trust departments of banks and separate trust companies, which could be local or national in scope. Factors to look at in evaluating and deciding upon a corporate trustee include:

- The financial institution's fee schedule.

- Any minimum amount of trust assets it requires. (For example, I am aware of several national institutions that require a minimum of $500,000 in trust assets to serve as trustee while local institutions generally accept smaller trusts.)

- Whether the institution places limits on the nature of assets it will manage as trustee. (For example, will it retain and lease farmland or residential rental properties, perhaps retaining the services of a property manager, or insist on selling such assets to place the proceeds in marketable securities?)

- The institution's staff and internal procedures. (For example, what are the experience and credentials of the trust officers? How will the trust officer handling your trust be selected when the time comes? How frequently do trust officers change? How are beneficiary requests for discretionary distributions handled?)

In some cases you might consider naming a friend or family member and a financial institution as co-trustees with a clear division of responsibilities. The friend or family member can be a source of information and guidance on issues of family history and dynamics while the corporate trustee focuses on proper accounting of principal and income, investment decisions, taxes, etc. To be effective, this requires the co-trustees to communicate and work together. It may also increase trust expenses with two trustees being compensated.

In the case of minor children, it is best to name a trustee different than the person you name as guardian (discussed below). This is a safeguard to ensure the trust's assets are properly used for the child's welfare. For example, the trustee can agree to purchase a good practice piano and pay for lessons, but decline to purchase a new Porsche 911 Targa so the guardian can drive the child to piano lessons in style.

Finally, you should include provisions for the selection and appointment of a new trustee should those named prove unable or unwilling to serve. Also consider a provision allowing the beneficiary(ies) to replace the trustee, although any such replacement is best limited to a financial institution authorized to administer trusts to prevent the beneficiary(ies) from selecting an individual trustee whose primary qualification is an inability to say "No."

## Conditional Distributions

Some people wish to specify conditions (often called "incentive clauses") for a beneficiary to receive certain distributions. For example, a provision might direct the trustee to make a specified distribution of principal if the beneficiary graduates from college or to make distributions linked to the earned income of the beneficiary.

But be careful you are not "the dead hand from the grave" seeking to exert control long after you're gone. College is appropriate for some people, but if a child's interest and inclination are for vocational training and the pursuit of a trade, inducing that child to spend four or more years on campus to get an unwanted degree to obtain a pay-out is of questionable value. While linking distributions to the earned income of the beneficiary might be intended to promote work, it may also unintentionally devalue a less-remunerated occupation such as working for a non-profit organization that is the beneficiary's true passion.  Or what if a child suffers a traumatic brain injury such that he or she simply cannot go to school or hold a job?

In any event, you cannot specify conditions contrary to public policy for either trust distributions, devises or bequests.  For example, no matter how much you detest the person a child married, if you make a bequest like "$50,000 to my daughter, Mary, on the condition that she divorce Richard," the court will not enforce it.  In all probability, Mary will receive the $50,000 and remain happily (for her part) married to Richard.

## Selecting a Guardian

The guardian is the person designated to assume responsibility for the person (as opposed to the property) of any child less than 18 years old.  Although you can name an individual or a married couple, most often it is advisable to name individuals.

For example, presume you think your sister Barbie, currently married to Ken, would make a great guardian.  Naming Barbie individually as guardian (as opposed to she and Ken jointly) will avoid complications if Barbie and Ken divorce before or after the guardianship commences, or if Barbie dies, becomes incapacitated, or is unable to serve for any other reason.  If you think Ken is a great guy and would want him to be the guardian if Barbie cannot, then you can name him as the back-up guardian.

The choice of a guardian for their minor children is frequently the most difficult estate planning decision for parents to make.  The reality is you will think of no one who you believe could step into your shoes as a parent and do everything as well as you.  But an imperfect choice is better than no choice.  Do not become paralyzed and fail to make a decision because, if you die without naming a guardian, the court will still appoint one – just without your input. So it is important for parents to discuss the alternatives, make compromises, and reach a decision on who to name.

Consider making a list of important attributes you want in a guardian, such as shared or similar values regarding lifestyle, religion, education or discipline. When evaluating particular persons as a possible guardian, consider their existing relationship with your child(ren), whether they already have their own children, their age, health, and ability to do what you think a guardian should do, and whether their location will require your children to move. Also keep in mind that a guardian need not be family.

If spouses cannot reach agreement on who to name, consider making separate lists of your top five choices, then comparing lists and looking for common ground. It may help to focus the choice on who you think would be an effective guardian over the next three to five years. In five years, when your 8-year-old has become a teenager, you can revisit the choice and execute a change to your Will (called a Codicil) naming a new guardian if that is appropriate.

Discuss your plans with the persons you want to name as primary and back-up guardians and be sure they are willing to serve in this capacity. Taking in and raising one or several children is a major responsibility. Just sticking in the name of someone who later declines to serve when needed accomplishes nothing.

## Selecting a Conservator

The conservator is responsible for the minor child's assets that, for some reason, do not get placed in trust. It is usually prudent to designate the same person or financial institution as you name to be the trustee (if there is a trust), so that distributions can be coordinated to meet the child's needs.

As with the trustee, if non-trust assets may be significant, then naming a conservator different from the guardian can provide some assurance that funds are primarily used for your child's benefit rather than that of the guardian.

## Selecting an Executor

The executor is the person, bank or trust company that administers your estate by gathering the assets, paying taxes and other debts, and distributing the property to those named in the Will (including the executor and any trustee(s), if applicable). You should name several back-up executors. While Kansas law generally requires the posting of a bond by the executor, your Will may expressly waive this requirement if you wish.

Your executor's duty is to carry out the lawful provisions of your Will whether they agree or disagree with what you specified. If your Will says the 1972 Gran Torino goes to your neighbor, Thao, then Thao gets it regardless of what your executor thinks. You may wish to discuss this duty with a person you are considering as an executor and be sure they are willing to comply, particularly if the possibility exists that your estate may not require court-supervised administration.

## Coordinating with Insurance & Retirement Plan Assets

The distribution of life insurance proceeds is controlled by the beneficiary designation you made with the insurer. Most often, married couples each designate the other spouse as their primary beneficiary. If you name your children as contingent beneficiaries, then the proceeds will be paid directly to them – which may create the need for a court-supervised conservatorship if they are still minors – if your spouse has predeceased you or you die in a common accident. Therefore, parents of minor children should consider a contingent beneficiary designation – such as "To the testamentary trust(s) created under the residuary clause of my Will" – that will funnel the insurance proceeds according to their plan.

Beneficiary designations on retirement plan assets are also crucial. If you fail to name a designated beneficiary, the default provision of your IRA or 401(k) / 403(b) account may be to pay the benefits to your estate – often with the adverse result of accelerating the pay-out and taxation of tax-deferred proceeds versus the ability for a designated beneficiary to take distributions based upon their life expectancy. This makes it especially important to keep your primary and contingent beneficiary designations up-to-date on all IRA's and other retirement accounts. You should ascertain any existing beneficiary designation and obtain a form for changes, if needed, from the custodian of your accounts.

Estate planning needs to be comprehensive. Be sure you coordinate any testamentary distributions of your Will with both beneficiary designations and any non-testamentary transfers.

## Business Succession Planning

If you are a business owner and have considered or decided upon any business succession plan – such as a purchase option for a family member or key employee – then you should ensure any Will provisions regarding the business conform to your succession plan.

If your spouse has no interest in continuing the business, but your children might, then you could consider Will provisions that provide for your spouse while creating an incentive for the children to take over the business. For example, your Will might offer your children the option to purchase the business for less than its appraised value (with this still substantial sum going to your surviving spouse). If your children decide not to purchase the business or the option expires, then the business is to be sold to the highest bidder.

## Status of Adopted Children

The statutes on intestate succession specifically include children adopted as provided by law in their definitions of children and issue. In a Will, you may specify who is to be included in the definition of your descendents. In my experience, most people include adopted children, although they may specify that the adoption be completed on or before the child reaching a certain age, such as the child's 16th birthday, to ensure the adoption is really for the benefit of the child and not simply a means to obtain an inheritance. Some persons prefer not to include adopted children. This is entirely a personal choice.

## Contractual or Non-Contractual Wills

Mutual Wills made in pursuance of a contract and in consideration of reciprocal provisions are valid in Kansas. Joint, mutual, and contractual Wills between spouses create a binding, enforceable obligation upon the survivor who takes under the Will to distribute the survivor's estate in accordance with the terms of the contractual Will.

Some people want to lock-in the decisions they have made (possibly out of concern that the surviving spouse might remarry and leave everything to their new spouse who then excludes the children) while others want the freedom to revise their planning in the event of changed circumstances (such as one child being seriously disabled such that the surviving parent wants to provide a larger bequest to that child to account for medical expenses and lack of earnings capacity). Keep in mind that other Will provisions – such as the lifetime trust discussed previously – might address some of these concerns without the need for contractual Wills.

Although the burden of proof is on the person asserting a contract and a contract cannot be presumed merely due to reciprocal testamentary dispositions, spouses who are executing similar Wills should include a disclaimer of contract to make this clear if they do not intend contractual Wills. Conversely, if your intent is to create contractual Wills, then this should be unambiguously stated.

## Homestead & Family Allowances / Spousal Elective Share

Kansas law makes specific provisions for a surviving spouse and minor children. For example, a surviving spouse has the right to elect to take a percentage of the decedent's augmented estate instead of what he or she would receive under the terms of the Will. This percentage increases based on the length of time the decedent and surviving spouse had been married, reaching a maximum of 50% at 15 years or more of marriage.

If circumstances are such that one or both spouses wish to create Wills leaving less than these statutory amounts to the other, then the other spouse must execute a voluntary, knowledgeable waiver of his or her right of election for the lesser share to be effective and binding.

## Safeguarding Your Will

Always safeguard your original Will and ensure your fiduciaries know its location as, should probate administration be needed, it is the original Will that must be submitted to the court. Options include a fireproof safe at home or a safe deposit box.

If the safe deposit box is held in joint tenancy and you die leaving a surviving joint tenant, that person can still access the safe deposit box. As a protection for the surviving joint tenant, the contents of the safe deposit box should be inventoried in the presence of a disinterested witness the first time it is opened after the decedent's death. This safeguard would also apply to entering a fireproof safe at home or any other location where the original Will is stored.

If you were the sole lessee of the safe deposit box or all joint lessees are deceased, then the box can be opened (by force, if necessary) in the presence of those persons claiming to be interested in the contents and two employees of the bank, one of whom must be an officer. The bank employees will then remove all documents of a testamentary nature and deposit them with the district court. At the bank employees' discretion, they may deliver life insurance policies to the named beneficiary(ies) and any deed to a cemetery lot and burial instructions to the appropriate persons. All other contents of the safe deposit box are retained by the bank and are to be delivered only to the parties legally entitled to them.

If your original Will cannot be found, this creates the presumption you revoked or destroyed it. While this presumption might be overcome and the terms of your Will established by clear and convincing evidence if the original cannot be found, the effort to do so will add substantially to the expense of administration while there is no guarantee it can be accomplished. So safeguard the original.

# REVOCABLE LIVING TRUSTS

The essence of a trust is that it separates the legal ownership and beneficial enjoyment of property. In the case of a Revocable Living Trust, the same person typically acts as the grantor transferring the legal title of property to the trust, the trustee managing the trust property according to the terms of the trust agreement, and the beneficiary enjoying the use and income of the trust's property.

For example, assume John Smith executed a trust agreement on January 15, 2013, creating the John Smith Trust and naming himself as its initial trustee. John would execute a General Assignment transferring his property to the Trust. If he owns real estate, John should also execute a deed in which he acts as the grantor conveying and warranting the real estate to "John Smith, Trustee of the John Smith Trust dated January 15, 2013, and his Successor Trustees" as the grantee. John would similarly re-title his motor vehicles in the name of the Trust (the Kansas DMV has a form, TR-81, Certification of Trust, for this purpose), change the ownership of all his financial accounts to the Trust, etc. This is called funding the Trust.

You should also notify your insurers that your Trust is now the legal owner of your house, motor vehicles, and any other insured property. While this should not affect your premiums as no underwriting factors have changed (after all, you're still the one driving your car), best practice would be to check with your insurers before creating the Trust to verify their procedures and determine if transferring property to a trust will have any impact on your coverage or premiums.

Note:  IRA's, 401(k)'s, 403(b)'s, and other retirement accounts are not transferred to the Trust as the IRS would view this as a taxable distribution and transfer.  Post-death distribution of these assets should avoid probate via their beneficiary designations.

After the property is transferred to the Trust, John still lives in his house and drives his car.  If he sells his house, he conveys the property via a Trustee's Deed that he signs in his capacity as trustee.  He can spend the interest earned by the Trust's bank accounts and any gains on the stocks, bonds, mutual funds, ETF's, or other financial assets it owns.  This is his beneficial enjoyment of the property as the Trust's beneficiary.  The Trust is invisible for tax purposes; all income is reported under John's social security number and he continues to file individual tax returns.

To document the existence of his Trust to any third parties, John would use an acknowledged Certificate of Trust.  The Certificate outlines certain aspects of the Trust, but omits any of the provisions for distribution at death to keep these private.

A Living Trust may contain any and all provisions for the distribution of property at death that a Will might have, including the creation of testamentary trusts.  However, there is no need for probate since John is not the legal owner of any property.  The Trust owns the property and the Trust continues to exist after his death, although its provisions become irrevocable at that time.  When John dies, the person he named as his successor trustee will take over with all the same powers and authority John held as trustee.  The successor trustee will act much like an executor in paying final expenses and debts, then distributing the property according to the Trust's instructions.  If the Trust owns real estate, the successor trustee simply conveys the property using a Trustee's Deed without any need for a court order assigning its title.

Unlike a Will, the Trust Agreement is not submitted for probate and there is no court supervision of the successor trustee's actions. Many people consider this privacy a benefit. However, depending upon the family dynamics, some may prefer the oversight and accountability of probate.

Note: While probably not an issue for us non-celebrities, probate filings are truly public records. For example, enter "Whitney Houston's Last Will and Testament" as a Google query and several links will provide you with a scanned image of her initial Will executed on February 3, 1993, and its Codicil signed on April 14, 2000. (Incidentally, Whitney opted for a testamentary trust with distributions at ages 21, 25, and 30.)

This process works smoothly so long as John ensured all property was held in the name of the Trust. If any significant property was not titled in the name of the Trust – for example, if John transferred his house to the Trust but forgot to transfer the ownership of some farmland in western Kansas that he visits once a year to go pheasant hunting with friends – then that property will require probate.

For this reason, even if you opt for a Living Trust you should have a short Pour-Over Will. This serves as a safety net to catch any property inadvertently left out of the Trust and provide that such property should be distributed according to the terms of the Trust. If there is any possibility of property having been left out of the Trust, best practice would be to file the Pour-Over Will with the court within six months of the grantor's death to preserve it. See the discussion of K.S.A. § 59-618a in the chapter on Estate Administration.

A Living Trust also creates an effective framework for the management of your affairs while you are still living if age or a loss of capacity warrants. To do so, you include provisions in the Trust specifying the conditions under which you are to be considered incapacitated and naming one or more successor trustees to handle your affairs during your incapacity. A stringent standard, requiring affidavits by two physicians, might read as follows:

> I shall be deemed disabled if two physicians, licensed to practice in the state in which I then reside, provide affidavits stating that each has personally examined me, and that my ability to receive and evaluate relevant information, or to effectively communicate decisions, or both, even with the use of assistive technologies or other supports, is impaired to such a degree that I lack the capacity to manage my property and affairs, or to meet essential needs for my health, safety, or welfare.

As a successor trustee, the person(s) you name would have the same power and authority to buy, sell, and manage the Trust's property as you (unless you include limitations on their power in the Trust Agreement). You remain the beneficiary of your Trust and the successor trustee is to act in a fiduciary capacity on your behalf. If you regain capacity, then you can resume acting as your own trustee.

You can also name one or more persons to serve with you as co-trustees or to take over as successor trustees even if you still possess capacity. My step-father is 97 and has little energy. My mother is 87 and nearly blind from macular degeneration. Although both are cogent and possess capacity, several years ago they added my sister and me as co-trustees of the Revocable Living Trust they had created in 1998. We now handle their day-to-day financial affairs – for example, their pharmacy in Florida mails the monthly bill to me and I write a check on the Trust's account to pay it – while keeping them informed and getting their input as needed.

A successor or co-trustee will possess significant authority and control over your financial affairs. I can just as easily write a check to myself as to the pharmacy in Florida. Unless I had a valid claim to the money, it would be theft – but theft difficult to prevent or detect. You want to be very confident you can trust a successor or co-trustee with such power, as discussed regarding the selection of an Attorney-in Fact in the chapter on Durable General Powers of Attorney.

A married couple may opt to have separate Living Trusts or a joint Living Trust. If a joint Trust, the surviving spouse typically continues as a trustee of the ongoing Trust after the death of the first-to-die spouse and the execution of that spouse's dispositive instructions.

A Living Trust can complicate matters if one spouse needs to qualify for Medicaid to pay for long-term nursing care. (Contrary to common belief, Medicare provides very limited coverage for such care.) Medicaid is a means-tested welfare program for which the applicant must meet strict income and asset requirements. In addition to a spousal set-aside of assets prior to a "spend-down" until the applicant has only $2,000 in assets remaining, certain assets – such as the primary residence where the community spouse will remain living – are exempt assets. However, these assets lose their exempt status if held by a trust. Therefore, be prepared to remove assets from a Living Trust and have them revert to individual ownership to obtain exempt status if the need for Medicaid funding of long-term nursing care arises.

Whether you have a Will, Living Trust, or no plan at all, Medicaid also applies a 5-year look-back period from the time you apply and are otherwise eligible to see if you transferred any assets for less than adequate consideration – made gifts – to anyone other than a spouse during that period. Basically, Medicaid wants to see if you became "poor" by giving property away. If so, a transfer penalty is calculated by dividing the total dollar amount of these gifts over the 5-year period by the current average daily rate that Medicaid pays for nursing home care to determine the number of days you will be denied benefits.

For example, four years ago you gave one of your children $10,000 to help with the down payment on a house and two years ago you gave a car with a market value of $5,000 to a grandchild. If these transfers cannot be cured by having the $15,000 restored to you, then at the current penalty divisor of $166.43 per day, Medicaid will impose an ineligibility penalty of 90 days ($15,000 ÷ $166.43 / day = 90.128 ~ 90 days.) The penalty also applies to gifts you made to a church or a charity. It even applies to actions you may have taken that prevented you from receiving property, such as the disclaimer of an inheritance.

As written, the Medicaid statutes and regulations apply the 5-year look-back period to all gifts regardless of their amount. In current practice, the focus is on larger gifts whose amount indicates the intent to transfer assets. However, the demographics of an aging population with an increasing need for long-term nursing care will only exacerbate the pressure on public funding and may prompt a closer look at past gifts. So be careful if you foresee the possibility of needing Medicaid for long-term care.

Bottom line, Medicaid is a Federal-State program subject to statutes and complex regulations at both levels. It is essential that anyone with even a moderate amount of assets consult with an expert in Medicaid planning if the need for long-term nursing care might arise.

# NON-TESTAMENTARY TRANSFERS

Kansas law provides several methods for non-testamentary transfers of property after death:

- <u>Joint Tenancy With Right of Survivorship:</u>  The distinctive characteristic of joint tenancy is the right of survivorship.  When one joint tenant dies, the property descends to the survivor or survivors.  (Of course, when the last surviving joint tenant dies, there is no one for the property to descend to and the transfer of ownership must be determined by some other means.)  While people often think of real estate being held in joint tenancy, a joint checking account is also a form of joint tenancy.  Similarly, you can title a motor vehicle jointly (with "and / or" appearing between the names on the title).

  If you are planning on using joint tenancy as a transfer mechanism, then check the real estate deed or title to other property to be sure a joint tenancy exists.  On several occasions I have assisted a surviving spouse who thought property had been held in joint tenancy when it was not.  Not only has this led to an unexpected need for some form of probate administration, in one case the deceased spouse died intestate and the surviving spouse only received a one-half interest in the real estate with the other half split among the children.

  A caveat – Parents sometimes consider adding a child to their bank account or the deed on their real estate as a means of transferring the property at death.  While this may raise gift tax issues, the most significant concern is that if the child added to the bank account or deed is later involved in bankruptcy or divorce, your bank account and your real estate may be included among the child's assets at issue. Plus, once you make a child a joint owner, you cannot remove them from ownership, refinance or sell the property without that child's consent. And, even if all goes well, at your death the property passes only to the child added as a joint tenant to the exclusion of any other children.

Note: If you want to add a child to an account for the convenience of writing checks and assisting you in handling your finances, this can be accomplished via a power of attorney without making the child a joint owner.

- Transfer-on-Death (TOD) Deed: A TOD Deed must be in writing, identify the grantee beneficiary(ies) and the property, be acknowledged by the present owner(s), and be recorded prior to the death of the owner(s) with the Register of Deeds in the county where the real estate is located. You can name alternate grantee beneficiary(ies) in case the primary grantee beneficiary(ies) do not survive you (which can be important as the transfer lapses if the primary dies before you and you have not designated an alternate).

  A TOD Deed can be revoked at any time by the filing of another TOD Deed (naming different beneficiaries) or the filing of a Revocation with the Register of Deeds. However, a TOD Deed may not be revoked by the provisions of a Will.

  At the death of the owner (who may be the last surviving joint tenant), the grantee beneficiaries may document the death and resulting transfer of the property by filing an official Death Certificate or an

Affidavit of Death & Survivorship with the Register of Deeds. The Affidavit is recommended as a Death Certificate contains a trove of information (full social security number, date and place of birth, parents' full names, etc.) that could be used for identity theft.

- <u>Transfer-on-Death Titling of Motor Vehicles:</u> A motor vehicle may be titled in TOD form by including in the Certificate of Title a designation of a beneficiary or beneficiaries to whom the vehicle shall be transferred on the death of the owner(s). After your death, the beneficiary(ies) complete Kansas DMV Form TR-82, Transfer on Death Affidavit, and take the completed Affidavit and other documentation to the County Treasurer's office to make application for the new Certificate of Title.

- <u>Pay-on-Death Designations of Deposit Accounts:</u> The owner of a deposit account (such as checking, savings, money market or certificate of deposit) at any bank, credit union, or savings and loan located in Kansas may specify that the balance of the account, or the owner's legal share of the account, be paid at their death to one or more beneficiaries.

- <u>Transfer-on-Death Registration of Securities Accounts:</u> A registering entity that originates or transfers a security title by registration may offer to accept registrations in beneficiary form and, if so, establish the terms and conditions under which it will do so.

- <u>Beneficiary Designations:</u> Distributions of life insurance proceeds, annuities, deferred compensation / pension plans, retirement accounts (such as an IRA, 401(k) or 403(b)), and 529 Plan accounts are typically controlled by the beneficiary designation on file. Be sure these are up-to-date and coordinated with other aspects of your estate plan.

Warning – By law, if you are divorced after making a Will, all provisions in that Will for the spouse from whom you are divorced are revoked. However, if you don't update the beneficiary designation on your life insurance, then your insurer will pay your ex-spouse at your death. The same would be true for any other assets controlled by a beneficiary designation you failed to update.

Unlike adding a person as a joint tenant, Transfer- or Pay-on-Death and beneficiary designations do not transfer any ownership interest to the beneficiary until the death of the owner. Neither do they affect the ability of the owner to sell, mortgage or take any other action with the property.

If you have set-up a non-testamentary transfer and later wish to alter its provisions, then you must do so using the proper procedure for that non-testamentary transfer. For a TOD Deed, you must file another TOD Deed (naming different beneficiaries) or file a Revocation with the Register of Deeds. For a bank account with a pay-on-death designation, you must go back to the bank and complete its paperwork to change or remove the designation. And so on. An unrevoked non-testamentary transfer will not be altered by a differing distribution provided for in a Will or Living Trust.

The shortcoming with non-testamentary transfers is that they work best only when people die in the "expected order." But this does not always occur. For example, if you name your child the beneficiary of a TOD Deed and then your child dies before you, or you and your child die in a common accident, the transfer will lapse. The same thing happens if joint tenants die together. And an inheritance, lottery win, settlement or other receipt of property too soon before your death to arrange for its disposition is always a possibility.

Thus, while potentially useful, non-testamentary transfers lack flexibility and are an incomplete substitute for a Will or Trust. The best practice would be to have at least a simple Will which can act as a safety net in the event a transfer lapses or you have a windfall just before you die.

# VIRTUAL ASSETS

Most assets have substance. You can see them, pick them up, and hand them to another person. But increasingly, we possess virtual assets that exist as electronic information – digital photographs, email accounts, social media such as Facebook or LinkedIn, electronic banking and brokerage accounts, etc. Access to these assets is often protected by passwords (that may change periodically) and the ability to answer security questions (What was the name of your first pet?). If you are incapacitated or die, how will people know these virtual assets exist and be able to access them?

Information regarding virtual assets changes too quickly to allow inclusion in a Will or Trust. Plus, remember that a Will is typically filed with the probate court and becomes a public document. That hardly promotes the security of passwords.

One option is to create a Virtual Asset Instruction Letter (VAIL) that identifies each account and its website, your user name and password, and the answers to any security questions, plus instructs your representative what you want done with it. Pay particular attention to any online financial accounts that do not mail you paper statements or recurring bills you pay online. Also be sure to include virtual assets that are not internet-based, such as those stored on your computer's hard drive or flash memory devices, and any passwords that protect access to these files. Update your VAIL as accounts and passwords change (one option is to keep the information on a CD or thumbdrive) and ensure it is stored in a secure location known to your representative.

While the VAIL is intended to ensure the identification of and access to your virtual assets, it is not a testamentary document. If there are virtual assets you own and want distributed to certain beneficiaries – such as an internet domain name you own – then these assets should be addressed in your Will or Trust like other property. For example, your Will or Trust might bequeath your ownership of the domain name "www.XYZCorp.com" to one of your children while your VAIL contains any password, security questions, and related information the child will need to access and control the website.

A complicating factor is that you may not own certain virtual assets. If you purchase a CD of an album by your favorite band, it's yours. If you pay to download a copy of the same album to an electronic device, you probably obtained only a nontransferable license to use the content of the digital file. For example, Amazon's terms of use specify: "You do not acquire any ownership rights in the software or music content."

You should also check the terms of use (you know, the ones you scrolled through as quickly as possible in order to click "I Agree" at the bottom back when you created the account) to verify how each company with which you hold an account handles it when you die. Terms of use vary, but are frequently written to preserve and protect the privacy of the deceased user. For example, upon being notified a user is dead, Facebook provides the option to "memorialize" the decedent's account with the ability of confirmed friends to continue posting messages. On the other hand, Yahoo!'s Terms of Service (last updated on November 24, 2008) include the following:

> No Right of Survivorship and Non-Transferability. You agree that your Yahoo! account is non-transferable and any rights to

your Yahoo! ID or contents within your account terminate upon your death. Upon receipt of a copy of a death certificate, your account may be terminated and all contents therein permanently deleted.

However, the *Wall Street Journal* recently quoted a Yahoo! representative as stating that "users need to provide consent and their account information in their estate plans" in order to be sure their account gets transferred at death. Thus, Yahoo! will apparently permit such transfers despite the seeming finality of its Terms of Service.

The post-death transfer and control of digital assets is an unsettled area of the law. Current news articles – such as "Life and Death Online: Who Controls a Digital Legacy?" that appeared in the January 5-6, 2013, edition of *WSJ Weekend* (the source of the updated Yahoo! information quoted above) – offer insights into how particular situations have played out. The key is to verify and be prepared to comply with the terms of use for the particular accounts you hold.

# DURABLE
# GENERAL POWERS OF ATTORNEY

Say "Estate Planning" and most people think of having a plan for what happens after they die. However, we all face the possibility of incapacity prior to death. This could occur over time as you age, or quite suddenly if a severe accident leaves you impaired.

For medical decisions, you should have a Durable Healthcare Power of Attorney and Living Will & Healthcare Directive (discussed later). If you don't have a Revocable Living Trust that provides for a successor trustee, then a Durable General Power of Attorney can provide for the continuity of your financial affairs during a period of incapacity. (Even if you have a Trust, you will need a Durable General Power of Attorney to grant authority for such actions as the signing of tax returns.)

A power of attorney grants authority to a person (called your Attorney-in-Fact) to act in your name. While a power of attorney can be very limited in scope (for example, authorizing a person to bid in your name on a certain tract of land at a specific real estate auction while you are on vacation), for estate planning purposes we are generally looking at a Durable General Power of Attorney – a legal document granting broad powers to act on your behalf that continues in effect even if you are disabled.

All powers of attorney are powerful documents. If your Attorney-in-Fact makes the winning bid in your name on that tract of land, then you are contracted to complete the purchase just as if you had made the winning bid in person.

But the scope of authority under a Durable General Power of Attorney raises the stakes.

Under the Kansas Power of Attorney Act, a Durable General Power of Attorney can authorize your Attorney-in-Fact to undertake virtually any lawful activity in your name – buy or sell property, take out or make loans, vote shares of stock, sign tax returns, etc. Delegation of certain powers – such as making, modifying or revoking a Will, Living Will, Durable Healthcare Power of Attorney or Do Not Resuscitate Directive – is prohibited by law.

Some powers exist only if expressly stated and authorized. For example, while an Attorney-in-Fact can generally buy and sell real estate, the authority to give consent for the sale, gift, transfer, mortgage or other alienation of your homestead exists only if expressly granted. Other powers that exist only if expressly granted include the authority to execute, amend or revoke any trust agreement, to make or revoke gifts, to designate or change the designation of beneficiaries to receive any property, benefit or contract right upon your death, etc.

Before you name someone your Attorney-in-Fact, talk to them and see if they are willing to serve in this capacity. If someone first learns they've been named your Attorney-in-Fact after you are incapacitated and then declines to serve, your Durable General Power of Attorney may be little more than an impressive, notarized piece of paper.

While your Attorney-in-Fact is supposed to exercise these powers for your welfare as a fiduciary, abuses do occur and assets can be misappropriated.

Therefore, you want to be very confident you can trust anyone designated as an Attorney-in-Fact with its authority. (The same with anyone you name as a successor or co-trustee in a Living Trust.) While it is useful to name successors who can serve in the event your primary

Attorney-in-Fact won't or can't serve (for example, you name your spouse as primary and he or she is killed in the same accident that incapacitates you, or your primary Attorney-in-Fact is initially willing to serve but later declines), be sure anyone you name as a successor meets the same standard of trust. If you've named someone and later learn something that alters your trust – such as that person being convicted of a crime or exhibiting signs of financial stress – then consider executing an updated Durable General Power of Attorney that names someone else.

Another safeguard can be to exclude the exercise of certain powers outright (in addition to those prohibited by law) or to require that the exercise of certain powers requires the agreement of your primary and successor Attorneys-in-Fact. For example, you can allow your primary Attorney-in-Fact to individually handle most transactions while specifying that certain transactions – such as the sale, gift, transfer, mortgage or other alienation of your homestead (if you've included that power), transactions above a specified dollar amount, withdrawal of an amount in excess of the Required Minimum Distribution from an IRA or other retirement account, etc. – require the agreement of your primary and successor Attorneys-in-Fact.

When do you want authority to vest in your Attorney-in-Fact? One option is to make the Durable General Power of Attorney effective immediately upon signing. This can be helpful if you are fully cogent but have physical conditions that limit your ability to travel places to take care of your affairs. Another option is to make the powers "springing" – where they come into effect upon your disability. As with a Living Trust, you can specify the conditions under which you are to be considered incapacitated.

Some organizations, particularly government agencies, may require you to name a representative on a form of their own. For example, if you want someone to work with the Social Security Administration on your behalf, then you must appoint them your representative using Form SSA-1696. Similarly, for assistance in dealing with the Veteran's Administration you can appoint a Veterans Service Organization (from the list of those recognized by the VA) as your representative using VA Form 21-22, or an individual person as your representative using VA Form 21-22a.

Bottom line: If there is any particular organization with which you anticipate your Attorney-in-Fact will need to deal, find out in advance whether it will accept your Durable General Power of Attorney or requires another form.

# DURABLE
# HEALTHCARE POWERS OF ATTORNEY

A Durable Healthcare Power of Attorney authorizes your agent to make decisions regarding medical treatment if you are unable to express your choices (such as being unconscious after an accident). Unless otherwise limited, K.S.A. § 58-629 allows a Durable Healthcare Power of Attorney to convey authority to your agent to:

- Consent, refuse consent, or withdraw consent to any care, treatment, service, or procedure to maintain, diagnose or treat a physical or mental condition, and to make decisions about organ donation, autopsy and disposition of your body;

- Make all necessary arrangements at any hospital, psychiatric hospital, psychiatric treatment facility, hospice, nursing home or similar institution, and to employ or discharge such healthcare personnel, including physicians, psychiatrists, psychologists, dentists, nurses, therapists or any other person who is licensed, certified or otherwise authorized or permitted by the laws of Kansas to administer healthcare, as the agent shall deem necessary for your physical, mental or emotional well being; and

- Request, receive and review any information, verbal or written, regarding your personal affairs or physical or mental health, including medical and hospital records and to execute any releases of other documents that may be required in order to obtain such information.

Generally speaking, a Durable Healthcare Power of Attorney should be effective immediately, subject to the signer's right to make any decision about their healthcare if they want and are able to, in order to avoid any risk of delay in the power of attorney being deemed in effect. (If you are cogent and able to discuss your medical options with your doctor, the doctor is going to listen to you and ignore an agent who tries to claim authority under the Durable Healthcare Power of Attorney.)

The persons you name as your primary and successor agents are often family, but need not be. What is important is that they know you and your healthcare preferences well, and are likely to be capable of making reasoned decisions under some degree of stress. For example, assume you struck your head in an accident and are lying unconscious in the ER. Your brain is swelling and will suffer severe injury if it compresses against the inside of your skull. There are two treatment options – one to attempt to stop the swelling by administering certain intravenous drugs, the other to surgically remove a portion of your skull so the swelling brain can expand without compressing itself – each with unique risks and benefits. Your healthcare agent should be a person who can discuss your situation and treatment options with the doctor, then chose the treatment option the agent believes you would make for yourself if you could.

Other attributes of a good agent are a person who can and will advocate for you with doctors, hospitals, and other healthcare providers, and who can manage conflict within the family if it occurs. Given the possible need for time-sensitive decisions, you should not appoint co-agents who must agree on your care. An option to keep the familial peace while preserving decisiveness might be to name friends and/or family members in sequence, but include a provision similar to the following:

> I have named persons in sequence to serve as my agent for healthcare decisions in recognition that the choice among medical options may require a rapid decision by a single person with authority. However, it is my wish that whichever person is serving as my agent for healthcare decisions attempt to confer with my family members and reach consensus if time permits. In the absence of consensus, the person currently serving as my healthcare agent shall make the decision.

A Durable Healthcare Power of Attorney contains sections that allow you to lay out any special instructions you might have for your healthcare providers and designated agents and to place limitations on your agents. While the option you select for these sections may be "None," they are opportunities to more clearly communicate your healthcare preferences if you wish.

As with a Durable General Power of Attorney, talk with the persons you want to name as your primary and successor agents before designating them, and then provide them with a copy of your executed Durable Healthcare Power of Attorney so they can document their decision-making authority if needed. You may also wish to provide copies of your Durable Healthcare Power of Attorney and Living Will & Healthcare Directive (discussed next) to each of your regular medical providers and ask that they be placed in your chart.

Also consider keeping a current list of your medical providers, medications, allergies, and known medical conditions with your Durable Healthcare Power of Attorney. Such a list could be very helpful to your agent, particularly if they are dealing with emergency room staff who need immediate information on your medical history.

And such a list could also be very helpful to you as some medications are known by a variety of names. If an ER doctor asks if you are taking medication X and prescribes it after you say you are not, you might suffer the effects of an overdose if you are taking medication Y – which happens to be the same or similar medication as X, just with a different name. Having a written list of your medications for the doctor to read will alert him or her to everything you are taking by whatever name it is called.

# LIVING WILLS
# &
# HEALTHCARE DIRECTIVES

Any adult may execute a declaration, called a Living Will, directing the withholding or withdrawal of life-sustaining procedures if he or she is in a terminal condition. A Living Will must be in writing, signed by the declarant (or by another person in the declarant's presence and by the declarant's express direction), dated, and signed either in the presence of two disinterested witnesses at least 18 years of age or acknowledged before a notary.

The essence of the Living Will is contained in the following declaration (taken from K.S.A. § 65-28,103):

> If at any time I should have an incurable injury, disease, or illness certified to be a terminal condition by two physicians who have personally examined me, one of whom shall be my attending physician, and the physicians have determined that my death will occur whether or not life-sustaining procedures are utilized and where the application of life-sustaining procedures would serve only to artificially prolong the dying process, I direct that such procedures be withheld or withdrawn, and that I be permitted to die naturally with only the administration of medication or the performance of any medical procedure deemed necessary to provide me with comfort care.

A life-sustaining procedure is any medical procedure or intervention which, when applied to a patient afflicted with a terminal condition, would serve only to prolong the dying process and where, in the judgment of the attending physician, death will occur whether or not such procedure or intervention is utilized. Life-sustaining procedures do not include the administration of medication or the performance of any medical procedure deemed necessary to provide comfort care or to alleviate pain.

In addition to the Living Will portion, the declaration may include other instructions regarding your medical care, called a Healthcare Directive. These instructions can be tailored to reflect your individual wishes. Options include:

- Specifying those life-sustaining procedures to be withheld or withdrawn in the event you have a condition, disease or injury without hope of a significant recovery and from which there is no reasonable expectation you will regain an acceptable quality of life, or substantial brain damage or brain disease which cannot be significantly reversed (either of which circumstance may not meet the criteria of a terminal condition);

- Directing that you are to be given healthcare treatment to relieve pain or to provide comfort even if such treatment might shorten your life, suppress your appetite or breathing, or be habit-forming; and

- Expressing any preferences you have regarding hospice care or living your last days at home, rather than in a hospital or nursing home.

Your expressed desires for medical treatment supersede the terms of a Living Will & Healthcare Directive. ("Hey, Doc, I decided I want to be on a ventilator.") You can also revoke a Living Will & Healthcare Directive at any time, although this must be done in a specified manner.

A Living Will & Healthcare Directive is an optional document. Unless excluded from their authority, your designated healthcare agents would have the power to make decisions to withhold end-of-life care under a Durable Healthcare Power of Attorney. Some people prefer to also have a Living Will to preclude their agents from having to make such decisions. If a person has a Living Will, then their choices expressed in the Living Will should take precedence over contrary choices expressed by their agent. (Although anecdotal reports indicate doctors may be inclined to follow the directions of the healthcare agent standing in front of them even if contrary to the patient's Living Will & Healthcare Directive – a reason to be sure your nominated agents really know your preferences and are prepared to follow them.)

Look back at the language in the first bullet-point on page 60. What does "hope of a significant recovery" mean to you? Or what would you consider a "reasonable expectation you will regain an acceptable quality of life"? However complete and well-written, a Durable Healthcare Power of Attorney and Living Will & Healthcare Directive are most effective when you have taken the time to really discuss your values and preferences with your designated healthcare agent.

In addition, a Living Will only expresses your preferences if you are in a terminal condition. What if you are in a persistent vegetative state that is not terminal? Your healthcare agent can best act on your behalf if they know your preferences and what is important to you. Is it certain qualities of life, the length of life, or potential tradeoffs between quality and length of life? Nothing replaces talking in depth about real medical possibilities and the choices you would want made.

You or your healthcare agent may also need to take the initiative in talking to your doctors about your condition and treatment options. For example, if you have late-stage cancer for which chemotherapy is a treatment option, although death appears inevitable, you need information on the potential benefits, side effects, and other options to make the best decision for you: What will your life be like if you get the chemotherapy? What will it be like if you do not? What is your anticipated life expectancy with and without the chemotherapy? What are your options for comfort care and pain management, whether in hospice or via visiting nurses at home?

If a medical decision is not time-critical, ask for information on it in a variety of formats. This might be an illustrated handout you or your agent can read after listening to the doctor's explanation. Or ask if there are any multi-media resources – such as a video showing the procedure – you can view. While such resources may not be available, if they are then people typically gain a better understanding of something when they get information in a variety of formats.

Each person is unique. Some may accept the side effects of chemotherapy as a fair trade for whatever extension of life it provides. Others may consider a shorter life with comfort care and the absence of side effects a better option. And the choice by any particular person might vary if there is a particular event – such as the birth of their first grandchild – they want to live long enough to see. But you or your healthcare agent need to know all the relevant information about your condition and treatment options to make the right choice for you. Take the initiative in talking to your doctors to get the information you need.

# DO NOT RESUSCITATE (DNR) DIRECTIVES

A Do Not Resuscitate (DNR) Directive expresses your desire "that if my heart stops beating or if I stop breathing, no medical procedure to restart breathing or heart functioning" should be taken. In short, you will not receive cardio-pulmonary resuscitation or related revival efforts. A DNR Directive does not affect your receipt of emergency care (for example, the suturing of a laceration or the setting of a broken bone) or other care directed by a doctor (such as antibiotics for an infection).

A DNR Directive must be in writing, signed by the declarant (or by another person in the declarant's presence and by the declarant's express direction), dated, and signed in the presence of a disinterested witness who is 18 years or older. Unless excepted by religious beliefs and practices, the Directive must also be signed by the declarant's attending physician affirming that it is medically appropriate. The Directive can be revoked at any time.

Note: Given the requirement for an attending physician's approval, a DNR Directive is a medical document, not a routine estate planning document. However, I have briefly addressed it here as in proper circumstances it might complement a Durable Healthcare Power of Attorney and Living Will & Healthcare Directive.

# PLANNING FOR ADULT CHILDREN

At 18, your child is legally an adult. If attending college, you will find the school is more than happy to cash your check for the tuition but will not tell you your child's grades without his or her authorization. Similarly, if you call the dorm and your child's roommate tells you they were just rushed to the hospital after an accident, medical personnel may cite the privacy and disclosure safeguards of HIPAA in refusing to release information on your child to you.

While the average single young adult may lack property that warrants a Will or Trust, they should have in place a Durable General Power of Attorney, Durable Healthcare Power of Attorney, and Living Will & Healthcare Directive (if desired) in the event of their incapacity.

Note: These documents must reflect your child's choices, even if you bear the cost of their preparation.

# UPDATING YOUR ESTATE PLAN

A well-drafted estate plan should incorporate flexibility. For example, contingency provisions regarding who receives certain property if you are not survived by the primary designee and the naming of successors to serve in positions such as executor, trustee, etc. If certain portions of your plan are rendered moot by the passage of time (such as your minor children growing to adulthood, making the naming of a guardian unnecessary), then these portions are simply ignored without affecting the other parts of your plan.

However, it is prudent to review your plan every 3 to 5 years, and you should definitely review and consider updating your estate plan upon major life changes, such as the following:

- Death of a spouse, child, or other named beneficiary.

- Marriage, divorce or remarriage.

- Birth or adoption of a child or grandchild.

- Change in your distributive intent.

- Significant change in your financial condition.

- Death or changed circumstances in the ability to serve of persons you have nominated as executors, guardians, trustees, Attorneys-in-Fact or healthcare agents.

- Changes in the needs of your children, such as a different guardian for a still minor child whose character and interests as a teenager warrant a guardian different from the person you thought would be best when they were a toddler, or the provision of a Special Needs Trust for a child who has become incapacitated since your earlier plan.

- Significant change in the estate tax laws (if these affect you).

Also, be aware that Kansas law (K.S.A. § 59-610) automatically revokes your Will or portions of it upon the occurrence of either of two events:

- "If after making a will the testator marries and has a child, by birth or adoption, the will is thereby revoked."
  - o This is intended to protect the child – making you intestate so the child is entitled to a share of your estate under intestate succession – but may lead to the concerns discussed previously.

- "If after making a will the testator is divorced, all provisions in such will in the favor of the testator's spouse so divorced are thereby revoked."
  - o You still need to update beneficiary designations on insurance policies, retirement accounts, survivor benefits under a pension or annuity, etc.
  - o And execute new Powers of Attorney to replace any that name your former spouse as your fiduciary. Would you want the doctor to ask your ex-spouse if you should be unplugged?

Kansas law makes no provision for partial revocation of a Will. If you line through provisions and write in something else, make erasures, attempt to obliterate or destroy a part of your Will, or similar acts, then the court will attempt to determine the original content of your Will. If it can do so, the Will is probated in its original form with all the attempted changes ignored. However, if there is no proof as to the content of an obliterated portion, then your entire Will may be denied probate, rendering it ineffective to pass any property or make other provisions.

If you decide to change the provisions of your Will, you must either complete a new Will (revoking your existing Will) or execute a Codicil amending the terms of your Will with the same formality as your original Will. (This is a major reason for and benefit of including a reference to a Written Statement for the Disposition of Tangible Personal Property in your Will.)

A Revocable Living Trust typically specifies the procedure by which it may be amended or revoked. If you have a Living Trust, be sure you comply with its provisions.

A helpful resource is The Elder Preparedness Self-Assessment Tool (TEPSAT) – available for free at www.elderornot.com – which is intended "to encourage the 100 million Americans who are at least 50 years old and their loved ones to prepare for the elder years." The TEPSAT consists of 82 multiple choice questions on a variety of topics related to preparation for aging well, such as life expectancy, health and wellness, paying for medical expenses, advance directives and other estate planning documents, etc. After you take the online self-assessment, you receive an email of your results that includes useful background information explaining the correct response to each question.

Finally, giving "estate planning" an expansive meaning, you should periodically revisit the liability coverage on your motor vehicles. On most policies, this also determines the amount of your Uninsured Motorist / Underinsured Motorist (UM / UIM) coverage.

Current Kansas law requires minimum liability coverage of $25,000 per person / $50,000 per occurrence. If a person with minimum coverage runs a stop sign and severely injures you, $25,000 may cover the helicopter life-flight and first few hours in a trauma center. In all probability, a person driving with minimal coverage (or even without insurance) will lack assets available to compensate your injuries in excess of their coverage. Rather, their insurance company will offer to pay you the policy limit in return for a full release of your claims against the person who injured you.

However, if you have UM / UIM coverage under your own policy in excess of the liability limits of the person who injured you, you can seek additional compensation from your insurer. This requires strict observance of statutory notice requirements to your insurer and may still require pursuing a lawsuit, but could be a crucial source of additional compensation for your medical expenses, lost income, and pain and suffering. Thus, carrying higher liability and UM / UIM coverage may, in some circumstances, protect you in the event of severe injury and incapacity.

In my experience, the typical "umbrella" policy only provides additional third-person liability coverage above the limits on your underlying motor vehicle and homeowner or renter policies. However, you may be able to obtain additional UM / UIM coverage as a rider with the payment of an additional premium.

# INCAPACITY / AFTER-YOU-DIE FILE

While not exhaustive, the following is a suggested list of items to keep in a secure location for use by your designated representative in the event of your incapacity or after your death:

- Original of your Will or Revocable Living Trust and Pour-Over Will.

- Originals of your Durable General Power of Attorney, Durable Healthcare Power of Attorney, and Living Will & Healthcare Directive.
  - These are relevant in the event of your incapacity. While powers of attorney remain effective while there is uncertainty if you are dead or alive (the cruise ship sank and they are still trying to account for passengers), a power of attorney is ineffective upon your known death.

- Copies of any representation authorizations you have provided to the Social Security Administration, the Veteran's Administration, or any other entity in lieu of your Durable General Power of Attorney.

- Copies of recent tax returns.

- Real estate deeds, motor vehicle titles, etc.

- Any recorded TOD Deeds.

- List of all assets (financial accounts, securities accounts, and motor vehicles) on which a pay- or transfer-on-death designation is in place.

- Life insurance policies.

- Birth certificates, adoption records, marriage licenses, divorce decrees, military discharge records, Social Security and Veteran's Administration claims, etc.

- Contracts, lease or rental agreements, etc.

- Receipts and warranty records for major items.

- List of bank accounts, mutual funds, brokerage accounts, etc.

- List of pensions, annuities, IRA's, 401(k)'s, 403(b)'s, etc. along with copies of the beneficiary designations and instructions on how to claim the survivor's benefit.

- List of significant personal property.

- List of loans on which you are the debtor or creditor, including active credit cards.

- List of online accounts, user names, and passwords.
  - See the discussion of a Virtual Asset Instruction Letter (VAIL) in the chapter on Virtual Assets.

- List of the names and contact information for your financial advisor, insurance agent, accountant or tax preparer, attorney, etc.

- List of the names and contact information for significant persons in your life along with any notification instructions.

If you have preferences or instructions regarding your funeral, you should both discuss these with the persons you anticipate will survive you and write them out. Be sure the proper people know where to find your written instructions quickly so they can act upon them. (Keep in mind your family may not review your Will or go through the complete cache of documents until after the funeral.) Consider including a copy of the list of the names and contact information for significant persons in your life with your funeral instructions.

# ESTATE ADMINISTRATION

Whether a person dies with a Will, Living Trust or intestate, certain actions are needed for the orderly handling of their affairs.  These may include:

- Identifying and safeguarding the decedent's assets.

- Determining the exact ownership of these assets – individually, in joint tenancy, as a co-tenant, or by a trust – and whether any pay- or transfer-on-death designations are in place.

- Notifying the Social Security Administration, Veteran's Administration, and other organizations of the death.

- Reporting the death to any former employer that was paying a pension to the decedent and initiating the claim for the survivor's benefit, if any.

- Initiating the claims for any assets controlled by beneficiary designations, such as life insurance, IRA's, etc.

- Determining whether the decedent, or a previously deceased spouse, was paid any form of medical assistance (such as Medicaid) and notifying the appropriate agencies of the death, if required, so they can determine if there is a claim against the estate.

- Providing actual notice to known creditors, published notice to potential creditors, and paying the legally enforceable debts.

- Filing the decedent's final individual federal and state income tax returns.

- Obtaining a tax identification number for the estate and filing its fiduciary federal and state income tax returns if the estate has income in excess of $600.

- Determining whether the estate will be subject to federal estate tax and filing the return / paying the tax due if necessary.

- If the decedent left a surviving spouse, deciding whether to file a federal estate tax return to compute and elect taking the deceased spousal unused exclusion amount even if a return is otherwise not needed.

- If the decedent owned property in states other than Kansas (which no longer has an estate tax), determining if any of those states have an estate or inheritance tax and filing the return / paying the tax if necessary.

- Identifying the beneficiaries and ensuring the correct property goes to the correct person, including the funding of any trusts that will remain ongoing after the period of administration.

Depending upon the nature and value of the decedent's assets, Kansas law provides a variety of probate procedures should court oversight or approval be needed. These include supervised administration, simplified administration, informal administration, determination of descent, refusal to grant letters of administration, and an affidavit of small estate. The key is to identify the most efficient, least cost procedure that will accomplish what the estate requires.

Although a properly funded Living Trust will avoid probate, a complete distribution of property may still take time. K.S.A. § 58a-817 provides that a trustee "shall proceed expeditiously to distribute the trust property to the persons entitled to it, subject to the right of the trustee to retain a reasonable reserve for the payment of debts, expenses, and taxes." Thus, a diligent successor trustee will retain sufficient assets until the deadline for claims by creditors has passed and final tax returns have been filed.

Note: The general rule is that a Will must be filed with the court no later than six months from the date of the decedent's death to be effective. The law also prescribes penalties upon anyone who knowingly withholds a Will. If there is a Will, then it should be filed within six months either to initiate its probate or to preserve it for possible use (such as in the event of the subsequent discovery of property requiring probate). For the latter purpose, K.S.A. § 59-618a provides a mechanism to file and preserve a Will without initiating administration.

# CONCLUSION & NOTES

I hope this book has helped you determine what you want to accomplish – both after your death and in the event of your incapacity – and think through a plan to make it happen. But thoughts and good intentions are not valid legal documents. I encourage you to make notes, gather more information and consult with an attorney, if needed, think through your options and make decisions, then give those decisions effect with the necessary estate planning documents.

_____

_____

_____

_____

_____

_____

_____

_____

_____

_____

Made in the USA
Charleston, SC
26 June 2015